First Published by Evans Brothers Limited
2A Portman Mansions,Chiltern Street, London W1U 6NR,
United Kingdom

Copyright © Evans Brothers Limited 2005

This edition published under license from Evans Brothers
Limited

North America edition published by Chelsea Clubhouse,
a division of Chelsea House Publishers and a subsidiary of
Haights Cross Communications
2080 Cabot Boulevard West, Suite 201, Langhorne,
PA 19047-1813

United States Copyright held by Chelsea House Publishers

A Haights Cross Communications ✔ Company

Printed in China

Library of Congress Cataloging-in-Publication Data
applied for.

ISBN 0-7910-8178-8

Acknowledgments

The author and publisher would like to thank the following
for their help with this book:

Becky, Natalie, Linda, and Jason McGovern and Francesca
Smith.

Thanks also to the Juvenile Diabetes Research Foundation
for their help in preparation of this book.

All photographs by Gareth Boden

Credits

Series Editor: Louise John
Editor: Julia Bird
Designer: Mark Holt
Production: Jenny Mulvanny

LIKE ME LIKE YOU

Becky Has
DIABETES

JILLIAN POWELL

CHELSEA CLUBHOUSE
An Imprint of Chelsea House Publishers

A Haights Cross Communications Company

Philadelphia

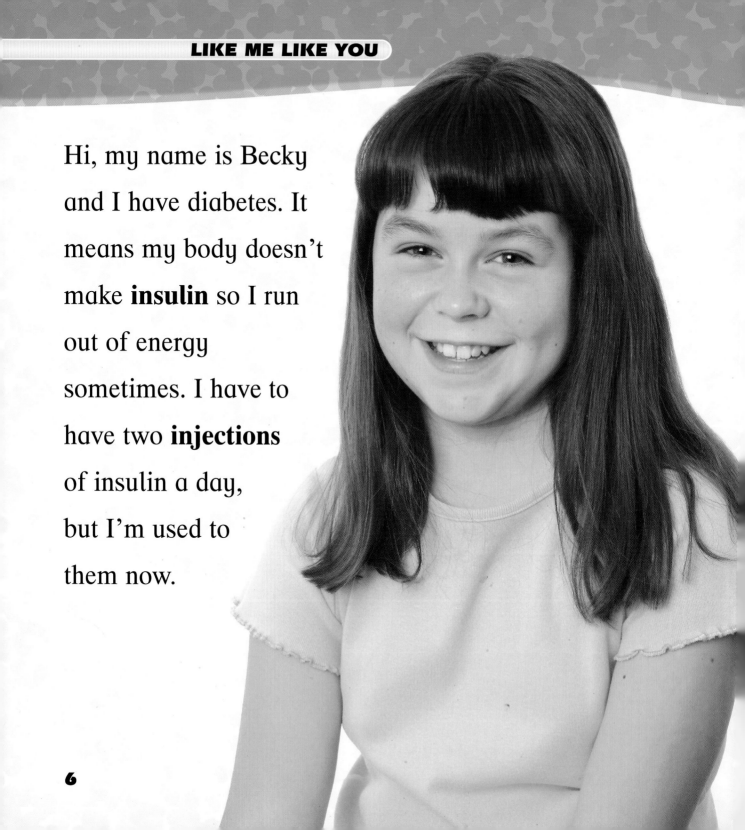

Hi, my name is Becky and I have diabetes. It means my body doesn't make **insulin** so I run out of energy sometimes. I have to have two **injections** of insulin a day, but I'm used to them now.

DIABETES

There are two types of diabetes. Children usually have type 1 diabetes, which means they need injections of insulin.

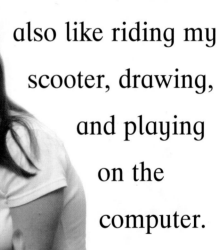

I live with my mom, my dad, my sister Natalie, and all our pets. We have two cats, a hamster, and two fish! I love animals, and I also like riding my scooter, drawing, and playing on the computer.

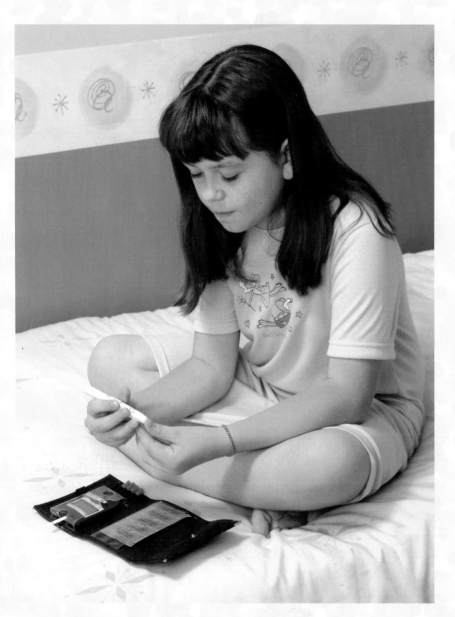

I share a bedroom with Natalie. Mom wakes us up in the morning. I have to wash my hands, then do my blood test. It's very easy. I prick my finger and squeeze a drop of blood on to the test paper.

8

The test tells me my **blood sugar level**. If my blood sugar level is low, I eat a bigger breakfast. I have to do a blood test before every meal. I write down the results in this book.

Now it's time for my insulin injection. Dad usually does my injections but I'm learning to do them myself. This morning I'm having the injection in my arm. Dad gives me the injection before he goes to work. I need to have it before I eat my breakfast.

My blood sugar level was okay this morning so I'm just having a bowl of cereal for breakfast. Because I have diabetes, I normally can't eat foods that have a lot of sugar in them. Mom always checks to see how much sugar there is in my food.

INSULIN

Insulin is normally made in our bodies. It helps our bodies use sugar from food to give us energy. When someone has diabetes, their body doesn't make enough insulin, so too much sugar stays in their blood.

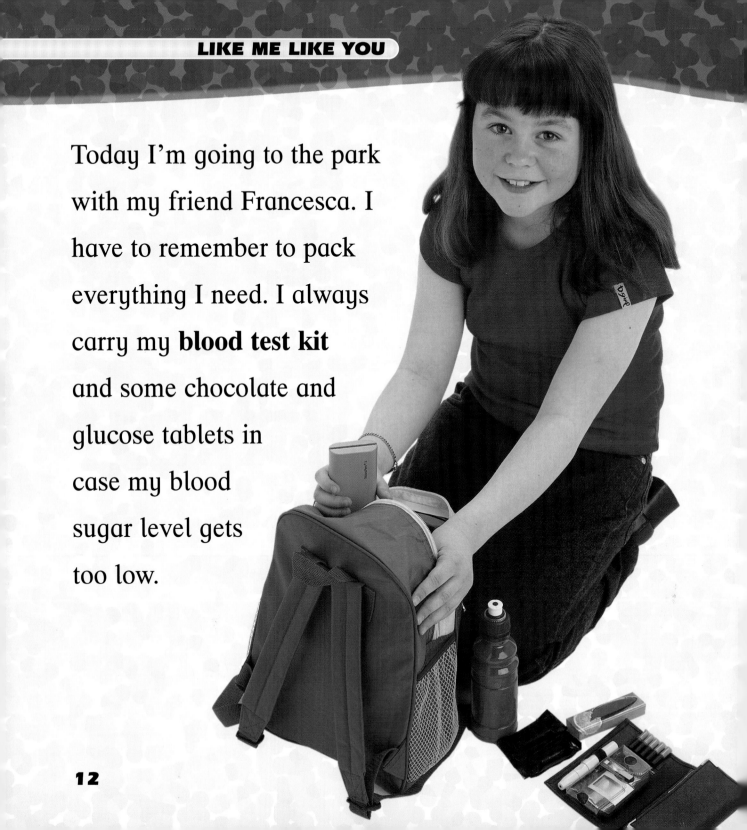

Today I'm going to the park with my friend Francesca. I have to remember to pack everything I need. I always carry my **blood test kit** and some chocolate and glucose tablets in case my blood sugar level gets too low.

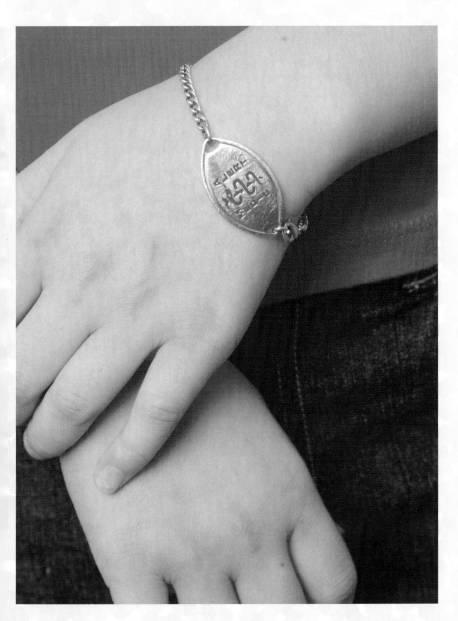

I always wear this special bracelet, too. It tells people that I have diabetes. If my blood sugar level got very low and I was ill, someone could phone the number on my bracelet to get help quickly.

Francesca's here! We're going to take our scooters to the park. We'll be using up lots of energy, so I must make sure I eat my packed lunch. I'll also have some snacks so my blood sugar level doesn't get too low.

Francesca always checks to see if I'm feeling okay. She's brought some chocolate bars in case I need one. But she tries not to eat too much candy in front of me because she knows I can't have them as often as she can!

Mom has packed me a healthy lunch. I've got cheese and crackers and a low-fat yogurt. I can eat most things, except for foods that have a lot of sugar or fat like cakes, cookies, and soda.

Today we're going to have ice cream for a treat. I can't eat ice cream very often because it has a lot of sugar in it. Sometimes I have a sugar-free lollipop instead.

On the way home, we stop at a shop to buy some candy. I keep some in a box at school in case my blood sugar level gets low. Francesca helps me choose some.

18

Francesca has to go home soon but she comes back to my house to see my new fish first. He's called Fizzle!

Later, when Francesca has gone, I tell Dad I'm feeling a bit **"hypo."** This happens when my blood sugar level is getting low. Sometimes it happens when I've been using lots of energy, but it can happen anytime— even when I'm in bed at night.

20

FEELING "HYPO"

When someone with diabetes feels "hypo" they may look pale and feel tired, dizzy, and shaky.

I feel dizzy and my hands get shaky. Dad tells me to do a blood test to see how low my blood sugar level is. He gives me some juice to bring the level back up. Then Mom makes me a snack.

Mom calls my teacher to remind her I have a checkup at the hospital in the morning, so I'll be a little late for school. I usually have a checkup four times a year.

I don't mind going for the checkups now. I know the doctor and the nurse. They weigh and measure me and look through my blood sugar results. We also talk about the best foods for me to eat.

Before I go to bed, I do another blood test. Then Mom makes me some toast so my blood sugar level doesn't get too low when I'm asleep.

I can sometimes wake up feeling a little hypo, so I keep a basket by my bed with everything I need inside.

When I first got diabetes, I was very ill and I had to go into the hospital to have lots of tests. I felt scared then, but I don't mind it so much now. I've gotten used to the injections and making sure I eat when I need to.

Having diabetes doesn't stop me from doing all my favorite things — like having water fights with Francesca!

Glossary

Blood sugar level the amount of sugar carried in someone's blood

Blood test kit a kit for testing the amount of sugar in the blood

Hypo (hypoglycemic) how someone feels when their blood sugar level is too low

Injection having a needle stick you to put something into the blood

Insulin a chemical made in the body that controls the amount of sugar in the blood

Index

Further Information

UNITED STATES

American Diabetes Association (ADA)

800-342-2383

www.diabetes.org

Provides information and support for people with diabetes, including message boards, a recipe of the day, a health tip of the day, and daily news and information about diabetes.

Juvenile Diabetes Research Foundation International (JDRF)

800-533-2873

www.jdf.org

JDRF offers information for parents, teachers, and others who interact with children and teens who have diabetes.

Children with Diabetes

www.childrenwithdiabetes.com

Online community for kids, families, and adults with diabetes. Includes chat rooms, recipes, and events.

Diabetes Monitor

www.diabetesmonitor.com

Over 100 pages of information are available, plus hyperlinks to other websites. Includes a database of answers to 13,500 questions, provided by an experienced team of diabetes health professionals.

BOOKS

Growing Up with Diabetes: What Children Want Their Parents to Know,
Alicia McAuliffe,
John Wiley & Sons, 2004

Matthew Takes His Shot,
Owen Coleman, Pentland Press, 2004

Understanding Diabetes, Marie Clark,
John Wiley & Sons, Incorporated, 2004

Diabetes: The Ultimate Teen Guide,
Katherine J. Moran et al.,
Scarecrow Press, Incorporated, 2004

How I Feel: A Book About Diabetes,
Michael Olson, Lantern Books, 2002